PAY YOUR STUDENT LOANS FAST

A PROVEN PLAN TO BREAK FREE FROM DEBT SO YOU CAN LIVE THE LIFE OF YOUR DREAMS

BY

VAL BREIT

Table of Contents

Bonus for You..i

This Book is for You If..iii

Introduction..1

Part 1: My Debt-Free Journey 3

Who is Val Breit? 5

Life-Changing Table 9

Graduating with Debt..11

Debt Annihilation...15

Life After Debt 19

Part 2: The Proven Plan to Get Out of Debt.................21

It Starts with You..23

Step 1. Lay a Solid Foundation 25

Step 2. Know Where You Are 29

Step 3. Know Where You Want to Go 35

Step 4. The *B* Word..41

Step 5. Hustle...Then Hustle Some More..........................49

Part 3: The Extras 65

Keep Learning...69

Stay Motivated..75

A Dozen Deadly Mistakes 79

What Will Your Story Be? 87

Grateful for You 89

Acknowledgments...91

Bonus for You

As a way of saying thank you for your purchase and time, I have FREE bonus resources exclusively for you, my readers. Everything you need to know to pay off your loans is in this book, but in the bonus items you will find my personal budget template and a cheat sheet to help you conquer the steps laid out in this book and get results even faster.

Visit Bonus.TheCommonCentsClub.com to access your free bonus materials.

This Book is for You If...

- You have student loans that you are sick of paying

- You are tired of throwing away money on interest

- You have things other than debt that you'd rather spend your money on

- You want a step-by-step plan to annihilate your debt

- You want freedom to do what matters most in your life

- You need a get out of debt plan that works without a six-figure salary

- You want to pay off debt without doing anything drastic, such as moving to another country, eating only ramen noodles, or living in the backwoods

- You want to be more confident handling your money

- You are committed to a temporarily hard journey to reap the massive benefits for the rest of your life

- You have an open mind to making changes in your daily life

- You take ownership of the choices that got you into debt

- You are ready to break free from debt and create the life of your dreams

This Book is Not for You If...

- You hope this book comes with a magic pill to erase your student loans overnight

- You believe someone else should be responsible for paying back your loans

- You love paying the interest charges on your student loans

- You are not willing to adjust your mindset or spending behavior to achieve a different outcome

- You are already convinced there is no plan that will work for you

- You like your student loans so much you hope to keep them around for decades

Introduction

Carrying tens or hundreds of thousands of dollars in debt has become commonplace, and student loans are a stressor for more than 44 million Americans. A life with debt may be typical, but it's suffocating. And it doesn't have to be your normal.

If you're like me, I'm guessing you dream of a life without financial worries, student loan payments, and wasted money on interest. You want to keep your hard-earned money and spend it on things that matter. Well, that is the goal of this book—to help you achieve that debt-free life.

I dreamt of the same financial freedom and found ways to wipe out more than $42,000 in student loans just over two years after my first payment was due. My journey to get out of debt made such a difference in my life that I want to share my experience with you. Hopefully, it can give you confidence and the tools you need to finally break free from your debt too.

As expected, rapidly eliminating my debt relieved me from the stress of having to come up with monthly payments. What I didn't expect, though, was how much *more* I gained from becoming debt-free. It allowed me the freedom to create a lifestyle I never imagined I could attain. A lifestyle that never would have been possible if I stuck to a standard repayment plan and kept my debt around for a decade or two. I now get to spend my time doing what matters most to me every day because I no longer have student loan payments.

What would change if you eliminated your debt? Do you long for a different life, maybe with more time to travel, more time with family, or freedom to pursue a different career? Do you feel stuck in a financial rut?

Many people feel like they will never get out from the burden of debt, but I assure you that debt-free life is possible, and it can happen sooner than you think. The best news? You don't need to earn a six-figure income or move to another country to repay your loans. I'll show you how to pay off your debt, so you can experience true financial freedom.

You'll find three main sections in this book. Part 1 is my story of getting debt-free, which proves that an ordinary person can do something extraordinary. Crushing my debt saved me $30,000 in interest and seventeen years of payments! How would you like to create statistics like that for your life?

Part 2 is the step-by-step plan of how you can pay off your loans in record time. This section will show you how to get from where you are to where you want to be. Although the plan focuses on student loans, these principles can be applied to any debt you'd like to get rid of.

Part 3 includes extra steps you can take to erase your debt faster as well as common myths and mistakes that get in people's way of paying off their debt.

I'm eager to embark on this journey with you. Let's crush your debt, free you from that burden, and start making your dreams a reality too.

Part 1:
My Debt-Free Journey

"Start by doing what's necessary; then, do what's possible; and suddenly you're doing the impossible."
- Francis of Assisi

Who is Val Breit?

Your Average Jane

So, who am I to be giving advice on how to pay off student loans? I am glad you asked.

I'm Val, and I'm just your average Jane. I am not a financial advisor, and I was not a finance major in college. I am your typical girl who accumulated more than $42,000 in student loan debt to cover expenses for undergraduate and graduate school. Then I became not-so-average and repaid all that debt in less than three years—on a modest public educator's salary.

Ignorance is Bliss

Here is a little background information: I did not receive or seek any knowledge of how to pay for college during high school. I never questioned if I would go to college, nor did I question how I would pay for college. They say ignorance is bliss, right?

I was responsible for paying for my own college expenses, and I used financial aid to fund most them. At times, I ended up receiving more financial aid than I needed to cover tuition, and I chose to pocket that money for books, rent, or other general living expenses. The advice my parents gave me was to "take as much as they'll give you," probably because of the misconceptions that student loans were at a super low interest rate and that they were "good debt" to help build my credit. In hindsight, I wish I had turned down every extra financial aid dollar on the spot. I had no idea what it would cost to repay.

I used almost all Direct federal student loans (which later became Sallie Mae, and later became Navient) and a small handful of Perkins loans. The interest rate on my loans were around 2% my first year of college, but the rate skyrocketed to 6.8% my second year. The interest rate remained at nearly 7% for the remainder of my college years. I was oblivious to this significant increase and what it meant for repayment down the road.

Through most of college, I worked 10-15 hours per week, earning a single-digit hourly wage. This small amount of income was spent on living expenses (rent, utilities, groceries, books, and entertainment). None of it went toward tuition. My logic was that since financial aid covered my tuition, why worry about it right now?

About halfway through obtaining my undergraduate degree—or I should say halfway through obtaining my undergraduate student loan debt—I had a mid-college crisis. I had a change of heart about my degree choice. After realizing I no longer wanted to work with juvenile delinquents, I began questioning what was I going to do with a degree in criminal justice.

I shadowed a local high school counselor. It sounded like a career in which I could use my gifts, make a difference, and earn a decent living. The counselor showed me their school district's salary schedule, and I focused on the number in the bottom right hand corner. I decided that wage could justify a few more years of college courses. So, I went on to finish my bachelor's degree, and after that I was off to graduate school!

I continued to embrace the strategy of using financial aid to fund the tuition bills. I made many decisions that at the time felt sacrificial and financially responsible (like moving back home with my parents for a while!), but it wasn't until later in graduate school that I understood the financial mess I'd created.

During all my previous college semesters, I applied for financial aid and was loaned the money through whatever institution the financial aid office chose for me. For some reason (that I still do not fully understand), this one semester in graduate school I had to select my own lender. This simple task ended up being a pivotal moment for me.

As far as I could tell, all the loan lenders were offering me the same amount of money, so I selected the lender with a mailing address closest to me. I do not know why I thought that mattered, but I had no reason to choose one lender over another. Little did I know, the bliss of ignorance was about to come to a screeching halt.

Life-Changing Table

The Pivotal Moment

So, I selected my lender and all was good, right? The story would typically continue with me trekking through graduate school with my head in the clouds, but instead my newly selected lender presented me with a hideous, gut-wrenching table of numbers that reality-slapped me in the face. This table was probably a government-regulated piece of information that often gets overlooked and tucked aside in the shuffle of loan paperwork. Fortunately for me, this time, that was not the case.

At this point, I was projecting to graduate with around $50,000 in student loans. I figured I would do the standard repayment plan, which was twenty years instead of ten because of the amount of my debt. This lender's brutal table showed me that it would cost nearly $100,000 to repay the $50,000 borrowed. *One-hundred-thousand-dollars!* After the shock, I burst into tears. The bliss of my ignorance was gone.

I felt like I would never be able to repay that amount of debt. I was convinced I would be paying it off forever. I would never get to buy a nice car, never live in a nice house, never travel around the world, and never have the American dream I had grown up believing was a sure thing if I obtained a college degree. I was compassionate and smart, had a fun sense of humor and good work ethic, and did well in school. I chose a career focused on helping others, and I was somewhat aware of living simply and not spending wastefully. Yet, what did I do wrong? How did I get myself into such a mess?

Small Steps

After coming out of my pit of sorrow and self-pity, after releasing anger over the fact that my parents could not help me financially and had not protected me from this mess, after letting go of the jealousy of my friends who had their entire college, rent, and food bills paid for all throughout college, I decided to take action.

That pivotal moment became the start of my "why." I could not change the mess I had already made, but I could start taking small steps to prevent this mess from turning into a complete disaster. For starters, I did not borrow a dime more than I needed to cover my final semesters of tuition. I bought used text books from a variety of websites instead of the grossly overpriced university bookstore. I worked a couple of part-time jobs and carefully planned my courses so I could finish graduate school as fast as possible. I saved everything I could and watched my bank account slowly grow.

Graduating with Debt

A Bleak Outlook

During graduate school, I moved in with my fiancé. After a long struggle, he eventually secured a teaching job, which required us to relocate and live on one income. In order to make ends meet, we had to be diligent with our finances to ensure we did not spend more than he earned.

As I was nearing the end of my graduate education, the state of Wisconsin made unheard of budget cuts to public education that put educators into a state of crisis. Districts were informed of multi-million-dollar budget cuts for the following school year, which meant "specialty" positions—like school counselors—were on the chopping block all over the state.

One large district, which serves more than 10,000 students in twenty-one different schools, gave pink slips (a notice that you might not get a contract to return next year) to *every* school counselor on staff. Some districts cut back to only one school counselor for the entire district. It was a disheartening time to be an educator.

And here I was, six-and-a-half years into my higher education for a degree that was specifically for *one* career—a career where experienced and talented people were losing their jobs like wildfire—with nothing but nearly $50,000 in student loans to my name.

How was I, a brand-spankin'-new counselor, ever going to land a school counseling job? How would I find a job close to where we now lived, where we had no

11

connections? How was I going to start earning enough money to pay back those massive loans and start contributing again to our household income? These thoughts were constantly in the back of my mind. I was worried. I was scared.

A Real Job and a Real Mess

A few weeks before my January graduation from graduate school, I interviewed for a rare school counseling position that extended through the remainder of that school year. I did my research, prepared as best I could, and I got the job! This was a tremendous relief. Finally, a *real* job with *real* paychecks.

And I needed it! Upon graduation, the loan mess I had to take responsibility for looked like this:

- One massive Direct loan I consolidated to $33,970.30 at 6.75%

- Two non-consolidated Direct loans of $2,625.80 at 1.79%

- One Perkins loan of $5,530 at 5%

I had a grand total of $42,126.10 of debt for my college education. This was the start of building my foundation. I knew how much money I was going to earn from my new job and how much debt I had to repay.

My Why - Money and Years

The thirty-four months following graduation was my student loan repayment journey. I got disgusted with my debt, set a lofty goal, and stuck to a plan until my loans were gone.

Below is a table like the one that shocked me into reality. I was filled with disgust at the "Interest Paid," the "Total Paid," and the "Years of Payments." Real numbers like these made me aware of how much it had cost me to borrow that money for college. I understood for the first time how interest worked, and it showed me how long I'd have to carry that suffocating weight.

Then I flipped my perspective to a glass half full, and added two columns of information to that table: "Years of Freedom" and "Money Saved." I took a serious look at that "Money Saved" column and asked myself, "What could I do with an extra $13,000? With an extra $32,000? An extra $97,000?" Answer: A LOT! This motivated me to see how much money I could save, and how many years of freedom from payments I could gain, if I sacrificed, got intentional, and attacked my debt with a vengeance.

Debt	Years of Payments	Monthly Payment	Total Interest Paid	Total Paid (Principle + Interest)	Years of Freedom	Money Saved
$30,000	20	$229	$24,960	$54,960.95	0	$0
$30,000	10	$345.24	$11,428.97	$41,428.97	10	$13,531.98
$30,000	5	$591.21	$5,472.54	$35,472.54	15	$19,488.41
$50,000	20	$381.67	$41,600.68	$91,600.68	0	$0
$50,000	10	$575.40	$19,048.28	$69,048.28	10	$22,552.40
$50,000	5	$985.35	$9,120.91	$59,120.91	15	$32,479.77
$75,000	20	$572.50	$62,402.38	$137,402.38	0	$0
$75,000	10	$863.10	$28,572.43	$103,572.43	10	$33,829.95
$75,000	5	$1,478.02	$13,681.42	$88,681.42	15	$48,720.96
$100,000	20	$763.34	$83,201.36	$183,201.36	0	$0
$100,000	10	$1,150.80	$38,096.57	$138,096.57	10	$45,104.79
$100,000	5	$1,970.70	$18,241.82	$118,241.82	15	$64,959.54
$150,000	20	$1,145.01	$124,802.04	$274,802.04	0	$0
$150,000	10	$1,726.20	$57,144.85	$207,144.85	10	$67,657.19
$150,000	5	$2,956.05	$27,362.72	$177,362.72	15	$97,439.32

Debt Annihilation

Teamwork

Although my husband and I always talked about our monthly bills and knew each other's spending habits, we did not have joint financial accounts until we purchased a home together. Once we went from an engaged couple to a married couple with joint financial accounts, then *my* debt payoff became more of a joint venture for us. When we combined *our* money in joint checking and savings accounts, we saw the bigger picture of how much money we had. Now, we were both new public educators, so our household income was modest. Regardless, we took the money we earned and became a more unified team working toward a shared goal. We talked about each bill and every extra debt payment along the way. He was my biggest supporter as we blasted away the rest of my student loans together.

Take Action to Make It Happen

After crunching loan repayment numbers, I created a detailed budget to look at our income and expenses. This helped me see how much money I could apply toward my debt each month, and how quickly I could get rid of it.

Then I set a specific goal targeting my biggest loan, which also had the highest interest rate ($33,970.30 at 6.75%). I used an online student loan repayment calculator and created the following table:

Years	Monthly	Interest	Total
20	$258.29	$28,020.66	$61,990.96
10	$390.06	$12,837.07	$46,807.37
8	$458.93	$10,086.54	$44,056.84
7	$508.56	$8,748.88	$42,719.18

(The calculator I used can be found at
FinAid.org/calculators/prepayment.phtml)

I figured out if I paid $460 per month for eight years, I'd repay about $10,000 in interest and $44,000 total. If, however, I stayed on the standard repayment plan (and instead let that extra money go toward things I *wanted*, but did not *need*), I'd pay $258 per month for 20 years. On this standard repayment plan, I'd pay about $28,000 in interest and $62,000 total! In other words, I could save $18,000 and eliminate twelve years of student loan payments! I felt as if it was worth it to dig deep into our budget and come up with the extra $200 needed each month. Although eight years seemed like a long time to make those higher payments, I could not fathom still paying for my college degree *twenty years later*, and I could not ignore that *$18,000* I could save.

The goal was set. I wanted to pay off my biggest student loan in eight years. Next, it was time to take action to make that goal happen. The first thing I did was set up the necessary automatic monthly payment.

Throughout the next year, I periodically calculated numbers to reevaluate our money earned and money spent. I was continually trying to squeeze every dollar I could out of our budget to pay even more toward my debt.

Even though I thought the extra $200 per month was all I could afford, I regularly found even more money and made lots of extra payments, big and small, one at a time.

Over time, I watched the loan balances dwindle. One by one, my loans began to disappear.

Boom! Outta Here!

During those years, I had countless moments of frustration. That I—the professional school counselor—was driving the junker in the school parking lot. That I had to ask to have said car jump-started...again. That we were making extra student loan payments instead of taking a spring break vacation. Many times, I felt as if I had a mountain of debt so big that I'd never see the light. Yet, we did it. And it was all worth it.

We completely paid off over $42,000 in debt in thirty-four months. All those extra payments allowed us to crush my eight-year goal. I still remember how amazing it felt to submit that final payment. And I still can't believe there was no confetti or party to celebrate. So instead I took a snapshot of my zero balance and added big red arrows, circles, and text, which read "BOOM!!! OUTTA HERE, SALLIE MAE!!" I sent it to my family to share the accomplishment. I was stoked!

How could I not be? By paying off the loan early and not sticking to the standard repayment plan, *we saved $30,000* in interest and *seventeen years* of payments! We were no longer slaves to the student loan lenders. We were free!

Life After Debt

It Gets Even Better

Saving wasted money on interest and gaining years of freedom were my motivators, but paying off my student loans early allowed me the freedom to create my dream life two years later.

You see, during one of my school counseling courses about careers, our professor was talking about doing what we love as a career. Someone brought up being a stay-at-home mom, and our professor appeared surprised by the topic. Here was a classroom full of ambitious, young women, most of whom were going into debt to obtain a master's degree, and someone's dream career was to be a stay-at-home mom.

Our professor asked the question, "How many of you, if money didn't matter, would choose to be a stay-at-home mom?"

I had never pondered this question before. I was not yet married at the time and nowhere near ready for children. But I'd always loved kids and after a few moments of thought I raised my hand, along with approximately half of our class.

That moment stood out to me as a "wow" moment. This is a dream most young women don't talk about in college, as they're hustling to advance their future career and income potential.

I hadn't thought about that class discussion much again until a few years later when my husband and I started talking about having our first child. At that point, I had two (college-educated) older sisters who were both raising beautiful, respectful, and intelligent children as stay-at-home moms. I admired them and what they were creating for their families. But financially, we needed my income.

By learning how to budget, live simply, and build savings, I was later able to take a gigantic leap of faith and begin my own business working from home. This allowed me flexible hours to earn an income in addition to being a stay-at-home-mom.

I had no idea when I was paying off my student loans that it'd help me later be able to live my dream. There is no way I'd be writing this book during my child's nap time, if we still had those loan payments every month.

But because we wiped out our debt, created a stable financial foundation, and practiced wise habits with money even after we were debt-free, I get to spend my limited time here on earth in ways that matter most to me. My daily schedule matches my values, and there's just something peaceful about that.

What would you do if you no longer had the burden of your debt? Getting out of debt will probably be a blessing to you in more ways than you can imagine. In the next section, we will dive deeper into the steps you can take to pay off your loans too. Who knows, maybe becoming debt-free is the start of creating your dream life too!

Part 2:
The Proven Plan
to Get Out of Debt

"A year from now you will wish you had started today."
-Karen Lamb

It Starts with You

Take Responsibility

You have debt. You may have borrowed the money for a good investment. Maybe, like me, you were a bit clueless about what all the numbers meant, but just like the legal principal goes: ignorance excuses no one. Owning your debt and admitting it's no one's mess but yours is a huge first step to getting rid of your debt.

Debt is nothing more than a habit of spending more than you earn. It's *your* habit. *You* spent the money. And if *you* don't change *your* ways, nothing else is going to change. You will continue living in your parent's basement, the bank will always own your stuff, you will throw away a sickening amount of money in interest and fees, you will never quit living paycheck to paycheck, and you will get to "retirement age" but won't be able to afford to quit working.

It doesn't have to be that way, even if that's the path you're on right now. *You* have a choice.

You can choose to take responsibility for the money you borrowed and you can choose how fast you pay it back. You can become one of those people you admire who paid off their student loans long before the due date. You can be the one who saved yourself years of payments and thousands of dollars in interest.

Giving all that money away in interest is as if you're flushing money down the toilet from every paycheck you earn. Seriously, why is a lifestyle with debt so common? This should be what our society considers weird!

5 Steps to Debt Elimination

The only thing standing between you and that final payment of your student loans is you, and a lot of little decisions along the way.

Here are the five key steps you can follow to wipe out your debt:

1. Lay a solid foundation

2. Know where you are

3. Know where you want to go

4. The *B* word

5. Hustle...then hustle some more

We'll break down each step into bite-sized pieces, with tips and examples, so you know exactly what to do.

Also, near the back of the book you will find even more resources that can help you as you implement these steps to eliminate your debt.

Step 1. Lay a Solid Foundation

Two Key Pieces

To get you started on the path to successfully pay off your debt, you first need to **lay a solid foundation** to build upon. There are two critical pieces of creating a solid foundation that's sure to see you through this journey to debt payoff: defining your why and building your support network. Without these two things, you'll have a shaky foundation. If you give each of these pieces the attention they deserve, you'll be off to a great start.

Define Your Why

The first—and perhaps the most important—thing you need to do is define your why. Why do you want to pay off your debt? What will you gain by having it gone? You must have a reason that is so valuable and meaningful that it's worth fighting for.

We all are motivated by and disgusted by different things. Do not move onto the next step until you figure out that thing you hate the most about your debt, and that thing you will love the most about being debt-free.

Perhaps your why is the financial stress you feel every month when the bills come in. Maybe you finally want to build a savings account with enough money in it to cover a medical emergency, to take time off work if needed, to buy a vehicle if yours breaks down, or to make a home repair when the next "oh crap" moment happens.

25

If you're married, maybe your why is to invest in your marriage. It's common knowledge that finances are one of the top reasons for divorce. Having a pile of debt and spending beyond your means is a recipe for financial disaster...which can easily spiral into relationship disaster. Getting on the same page as your spouse and accomplishing a goal together (like getting debt-free!) can strengthen your marriage and create a more stable foundation for your relationship in the future. Plus, if you can get debt-free together, just imagine what else you can do together!

Do you desire more flexibility to pursue a different career? Do you wish you could spend more time with family? Do you want to be free to give more to people in need or causes you are passionate about? Is it your dream to explore more of the world? Do you want to set an awesome example for your children? Or retire with complete freedom someday?

Whatever it is that gets you most excited about paying off your student loans will be your why. A few of these ideas may resonate with you, but I want you to take a few moments to get clear on exactly what your why is.

Next, write it down. Put it somewhere you can see it regularly. There are going to be tough days, and you're going to need to be reminded of why you're trying to destroy your loans. Without a distinct why, it will be too easy for you to try this for a while and then quit. But you're not a quitter, and your why is worth fighting for with everything you've got!

Action Step: Before you move on to the next step, pause, reflect, and answer these questions. These are crucial to your success.

I want to pay off my student loans because *(what is your biggest motivator?)*

_____.

When I pay off my student loans as fast as possible *(what will happen?)*

_____.

Build Your Support Team

Awesome! You have defined your why—way to go!

Next, you'll take that why a step further and build a team of support and accountability around you. Share your why with at least one person who cares about you. Having a team around you can bring support and accountability that will help you throughout the process. If you're married, your spouse should be part of your team. In addition, you may talk to a close friend, a parent, a sibling, or a co-worker. Heck, you can even talk to me about it!

When you tell others about your why, you may gain more clarity about why you're doing what you're doing. Your team will also begin to understand why they may notice changes in how you spend your time and money in the near future. Plus, you'll have people to celebrate with at each milestone of your journey, including when you finally conquer that seemingly insurmountable task of paying off ALL your student loans.

It's important that the people you rely on for help and comfort are supportive of your why. They shouldn't criticize or harass you about it. They shouldn't try to pull you away from achieving your goal by enticing you to spend money in ways that go against your plan. Your team should be people who help keep you on target and encourage you every step of the way.

27

I've also heard lots of success stories from people who took Dave Ramsey's Financial Peace University, which is a small group course and curriculum for getting out of debt. People claim being around others who are going through similar struggles and fighting for similar goals was crucial to their success.

Now, some of you might be thinking, yeah, right! You may be so embarrassed by your debt that you don't want to tell a soul. Maybe you've worked hard to appear like you have it all together and disclosing your debt would undo all that work. Please reconsider.

I think we'd all benefit if we started being more real and talking more openly about money. What people earn and how much debt they have are such taboo topics, and it creates a whole lot of people who *look* like they have it all together, but are stressed to the gills and in debt up to their eyeballs.

When you get real about your finances instead creating a false appearance, you'll learn, grow, and find relief in being authentic. Plus, you'll be even more likely to achieve your financial goals. That's why you're doing this.

Now take a moment list people you think will be most supportive and helpful to be part of your team. There may be times in the future when you're feeling alone and this list could help remind of you of just the right person to encourage you or hold you accountable.

Action Step: Some people who would be helpful to include on my team are

_____.

With your why defined and your support team around you, you have a solid foundation for your battle to eliminate your student loans.

Step 2. Know Where You Are

Three Questions

After you've established a solid foundation, the second step is to **know where you are**. Before you can get to where you want to go, you need to first figure out where you are right now.

To understand where you are financially, you need to be able to answer three questions:

1) How much debt do you have?

2) How much money do you earn?

3) How much money do you spend?

For some, the reality of these numbers might be painful. Nonetheless, you need to get through this uncomfortable step in order to get anywhere different. And we both know you want to be somewhere different!

How Much Debt Do You Have?

Here's how to figure out how much you owe in student loans:

1) Gather all your current student loan statements. Include loans that are in deferment or forbearance, too. Statements may be online or paper statements you received in the mail.

2) Locate the loan balance for each loan.

3) Identify the minimum payment amount for each loan.

4) Find the interest rate for each loan.

5) Write these three numbers down somewhere (notebook or spreadsheet)

6) Add up your total loan balances.

7) Add up your total minimum payments.

Note: You may have other debt besides student loans. You can apply these steps to any type of debt you want to get rid of. It might be overwhelming for some to consider a bunch of debts at once, so I focused solely on student loan debt—the debt millions of teens are getting into and over 44 million adults are still battling.

This should give you an idea of how many different student loans you have, the balance of each, how their interest rates compare, the total you need to pay each month to meet the minimum payments, and your total student loan amount. Now you know the debt enemy you're preparing to attack.

How Much Money Do You Earn?

Next, it's time to look at your best weapon: your income.

Another crucial piece of understanding where you are is knowing exactly how much you earn, or if you're married, how much you and your spouse earn. You may need to look at your pay stubs or bank account to see the deposited amount.

You'll probably want to calculate your average monthly income and your annual income. This helps you see a snapshot of the month, as well as the overall picture of a year. Write your income in a separate space on your debt worksheet where you can easily find it again.

After you calculate your monthly income, compare it to the total minimum amount due you calculated previously. Hopefully you earn quite a bit more each month than you need to cover the minimum payments of your loans. Given your monthly income, should you be able to pay more than the minimum required payment?

Next, compare your total annual income to your total debt amount. Is your income greater than your debt, or is your debt greater than your income? Considering your annual income, is it realistic that you can pay off your student loans? Will eliminating your debt be an enormous struggle, or should it be manageable with some temporary sacrifice and intentionality?

These questions will help you understand how much money you have to work with as you prepare to attack your debt.

How Much Money Do You Spend?

After you figure out how much money you earn, you might be wondering, "Where does all that money go every month?" Or you might be thinking, "That's it...?" knowing you must spend more than that each month. This next step will help you understand two important things: how much money you spend and where your money is going.

We will focus on your spending one month at a time since many bills are due monthly. You can add "Expenses" as another page in your notebook or spreadsheet to go along with your debt and income figures.

You'll want different categories for dividing your expenses, such as Rent/Mortgage, Utilities, Groceries,

Student Loans, Vehicles, Gasoline, Cable, Internet, Cell Phone, Insurance, Clothing, Restaurants, Entertainment, and Savings.

To figure out how much money you spend, it will help to look at your bank and credit card statements. Instead of just documenting a general "Credit Card" category, I found it much more effective to categorize each charge on my bill wherever it fit (e.g., groceries, restaurant, clothing). I recommend you do the same. You will be able to more clearly see where all your money is going. This will likely help you find quite a bit of money you can later reallocate toward paying off your debt.

This may sound tedious and time consuming, and at first it is. But anything worth doing is worth doing right, and if you're serious about rapidly paying off your debt and gaining more financial freedom, then you need to thoroughly examine your spending. You'll never find more money to put toward your debt solely by reading a book. You need to do the work that's proven to get results: scrutinize your statements and track what you spend.

If this sounds overwhelming, just take a deep breath. If you've never done this before, it will feel awkward at first. But if you keep doing what you're doing, you'll keep getting what you're getting. If you want different results (remember your why), then you must do something different to get there.

Start with tracking last month's spending. Grab your most recent bank statement and divide all your purchases into categories. Then grab another statement, such as last month's credit card statement, and add those purchases to your categories. Continue putting your purchases into categories until you have gone through all your statements for last month. Then add the total amount you spent for each category. You can then add all the categories together to learn how much you spent on everything last month.

You'll want to repeat this process for at least three months to figure out your spending patterns. How does your total amount spent in a month compare to the total amount you earn in a month? Do you have a debt habit of spending more than you make?

Carefully tracking your spending is incredibly valuable information. Once you better understand where your money has been going, you have the knowledge to make changes and tell your future money where to go instead.

Keep It Real

After you act on the previous sections, you should know:

- How much debt you have

- How much you earn

- How much you spend

This is what you need for the big picture of your financial situation. Now it's time to keep it real.

Given your income, your expenses, and your amount of debt, how fast do you think you'll be able to get out of debt?

If you earn $20,000 a year and you have $120,000 in student loan debt, it's unrealistic to think you're going to pay that loan off this year—or even three years from now—without drastically increasing your income. No matter what book you read, those numbers do not add up.

However, if you earn $120,000 per year and you have $20,000 in student loan debt, man, I hope you destroy that annoying student loan this year!

When we get to budgeting and hustling (steps four and five), you'll gain new ideas for ways you can cut your monthly expenses and increase your income—both of which will help you pay off your debt faster. But I want to be real with you that this isn't a miracle pill. It's going to take some sacrifice and hard work. It's going to feel weird, but I promise you that it will be worth it!

Step 3. Know Where You Want to Go

Get SMART

The third step in achieving your debt-free life is **know where you want to go**. In this step, you'll be solidifying your goal. But as the quote goes, a goal without a plan is just a wish (Antoine de Saint-Exupéry).

Wish you were out of debt? Okay—keep wishing. See where that gets you.

Determined to get out of debt? Create a plan—and follow it. See where that takes you!

Goal setting for me is natural. I love doing more and seeing progress. But even if you're not quite as giddy as I am about setting goals, they're crucial to your success. If you want to follow a plan that's proven to work, take some time to set your goal.

Before you quickly set a goal like "I want to get out of debt" and move on, hear me out. Those vague goals are rarely achieved. Instead, take a couple of extra minutes to define a SMART goal. Setting SMART goals is...well, smart...because you're more likely to achieve them.

There are several different ways people define SMART goals, and here's my favorite:

SMART stands for:

Specific

Measurable

Attainable

Results-Oriented

Timely

Specific - What exactly do you want to achieve? Make it so clear that someone who doesn't have a clue what you're talking about knows exactly what you're aiming for.

Measurable - How would I know exactly when you achieve your goal? Make your goal something you can measure so it's clear when you meet it.

Attainable - Is it a goal that's realistic for you to attain? Make it a stretch, yet something you can do if you focus and work hard.

Results-Oriented - Is your goal based on the results you will achieve? Define what the outcome will be.

Timely - When will you accomplish this goal? Set a target deadline to put a little urgency in your plan. Using debt repayment calculators and your budget will help you set a realistic deadline.

As an example, my SMART goal was: *I will pay off my biggest student loan within eight years by paying $460 per month toward that loan every doggone month.*

You'll need to use the knowledge about how much debt you have, how much you earn, and how much you spend to figure out how fast you can pay off your debt. Using a student loan repayment calculator can help you calculate your numbers based on how much you plan to pay toward it each month. Or if you have a set date in mind, like a specific milestone in your life, you can calculate how much you'll have to pay each month in order to erase your debt by that date. Then you can change your monthly spending accordingly (aka budgeting...which we'll get into in the next big step).

Once you define your deadline, dollar amount, and how you're going to achieve it, you'll be well on your way to turning your wish into something you achieve.

You may find it helpful to set a short-term goal as well as a long-term goal. They should both be SMART goals, but small goals will help you stick to the plan needed to achieve your big, long-term goal.

Your short- and long-term goals might look something like this:

Short-Term Goal: *I will cut $200 from my expenses next month by cooking all our dinners at home (and avoiding Target like the plague).*

Long-Term Goal: *I will pay off $20,000 in student loans by next December by paying $200 extra toward my student loans every month.*

You can be modest if that's what you're comfortable with, or you can be outrageous if you know you'll kick it into high gear in order to achieve it. Just set something that's better than the plan you're on right now, and promise yourself that you will stick to it!

Action Step: To apply these steps, here is a simple goal template to get you started. Go ahead and fill it in. You might change it in the future, but at least take this step to get yourself on a better path toward achieving your why.

I will _____ (specific, measurable, attainable, results-oriented target) by _____ (deadline) by _____ (doing what? how will you achieve this?).

I am so excited for you to achieve your goal! When will you get to start spending for the future instead of paying off the debts of your past? Contact me any time to share your goals. I'd love to hear them...I like them that much.

Get Current

I should note that if you are in default or delinquency with any of your debts, your first goal should be to get current. This means get up to date paying any overdue balance and get in a position where you are earning enough money to make all your minimum monthly payments on time. It's not wise to pay extra on your student loan debt if you're three months behind on paying your rent.

If you're not yet current with your bills and you're not sure what to do, I highly suggest you borrow Dave Ramsey's *The Total Money Makeover* from your local library and listen to *The Dave Ramsey* radio show/podcast today. Both are free. The strategies in this book are applicable after you've become current and are looking to knock out your student loans fast.

Spread the News

Now that you have set a SMART goal, write it down somewhere. Heck, write it down in a few different places. Then place that awesome aspiration where you will see it so it can remind and inspire you daily. It can be big, bold, and bright or it can be written in pencil on a sticky note. It can even include a sticker chart or calendar dates to cross off if that helps you stay motivated. Do whatever it takes to visually remind yourself often what you're working toward and why.

Sharing your goal with others is another tactic proven to help people stick to a plan. For starters, you'll probably talk about it with those in your support team. Then you can take it even further. You can make your goal public through conversation, text, or even social media. You can share it with your close connections online or share it in a group that includes others who are paying off debt, like The Common Cents Club group on Facebook.

This allows more people to encourage you and hold you accountable for your decisions. Give others permission to check in with you and see how you're doing in a few months. Perhaps your support team will send you messages cheering you on or even sharing how inspired they are by your actions.

Ultimately, spreading the news will help you follow through with achieving your goal.

Step 4. The *B* Word

The Importance of Budgeting

The fourth step in this proven get out of debt plan is the big...bad...*B* word...**budgeting**! There are entire books and lots of online articles about budgeting. Most financial podcasts, personal finance websites, or even frugal mama blogs talk about budgeting. It is a topic that is brought up repeatedly because it works.

Budgeting is simply a process of writing down how much you earn (income) minus how much you spend (expenses). It's categorizing your expenses so you can see where your money is being spent. And it's the opportunity for you to tell all your money where to go.

If you tracked your spending for the last few months and don't like what you see, then budgeting for the upcoming month is your chance to tell your money to go somewhere different. For example, if you decide to cut your monthly $150 cable bill, then you have $150 each month to spend on something else. You need to decide where you want that $150 to go and make sure it happens. Likewise, if you discover you only have room for $30 to spend on clothing, then you know this before you step foot into any physical or online store. That's one pair of leggings, people. Not two. Not leggings and a shirt. $30, period.

If you don't have your income and expenses mapped out at the beginning of the month, it is incredibly easy to spend a little here, then go buy that over there...pretty soon you've spent hundreds of dollars on stuff you never intended to buy. We are bombarded daily with advertisement messages that we will be happier if we buy this product or that service. We are constantly tempted to spend money. Without a budget, and the discipline to follow it, your money will fall out of your wallet like confetti at the Super Bowl. And once it's gone, there is no way to get it back. Simply stated, if you don't tell your money where to go, you will wonder where it went.

Budgeting is going to be a key part of your master plan to get from where you are to where you desire to be. Even though my student loans were paid off years ago, we still do a budget every month. It's proven to be the game changer in accomplishing financial goals. Your budget turns a wish into a plan of action. That's why most financially fit people, even when they're long out of debt, still do a budget.

A lot of people get overwhelmed by the whole budgeting thing, or they avoid it because it's uncomfortable. Don't give in that easily. Budgeting is a skill you need to develop, so don't be surprised if it's awkward at first. It's only natural that you must practice the budgeting process and stick with it even when it's uncomfortable in order to get better at it over time. You'll learn a lot from trial and error, and it will get easier over time. You'll gain confidence in your finances, and you may even learn to enjoy budgeting!

If you're married, it's best to do your budgeting with your spouse. If you're not married, you can do it alone or find a supportive partner in crime to walk through the process with you. Sometimes just having someone there to listen or to ask, "Does that look right? Does this add up?" can be extremely helpful and build your confidence.

It also naturally invites some accountability by sharing your plan with someone else.

Budgeting is the best strategy to ensure you eliminate your student loans fast. Create and stick to your plan, recognize and resist temptation, and you will finally pay off your strenuous debt.

Budgeting Process

Budgeting is an ongoing process. Let's pretend it is May, and you want to begin the habit of budgeting in June. Here's what budgeting will look like:

Before the Month Begins

Near the end of May, set a budget meeting. Estimate how much income you will earn in June. Allocate every dollar you will earn to an appropriate expense category. Ensure your total for expenses equals your total income, and is not greater than your income. This is your financial plan, or your budget, for the month of June.

Throughout the Month

Throughout June, record your what you spend in the relevant category. Add your expenditures throughout the month to ensure you do not overspend.

At the End of the Month

At the end of June, it's time for another budget meeting. Review your bank and credit card statements to make sure you documented all your spending for the month. Fill in any expenses you forgot to track then add up your total amount spent in each category. Compare what you had planned to spend to what you actually spent. Then create your financial plan for the following month.

Throughout the month, something unexpected may happen. If you spend more than you planned in one category, then you need to spend less than you planned to make up for it in another category. For example, if you overspend on groceries, you need to reduce the amount you can spend somewhere else. (Hint: It shouldn't be on your debt payment...try looking at entertainment, restaurants, clothing, random stuff you find in the aisles of Target, or any of those other categories that are wants, not needs.)

If you get to the end of the month and realize you spend way more on groceries than you thought, you know this for the following month: you need to budget more and/or you need to spend less.

If you overspend in one category, and don't reduce your spending in another category to make up for it, you will continue to accumulate debt. This is the debt habit. There will not be enough money to go around (i.e., you will not be able to make the extra payment on your debt needed to achieve your goals). The math is simple. It's the disciplined behavior that's the hard part. Hard, but not impossible.

The process of budgeting will get easier over time. You will get used to recording what you spend throughout the month. You will more accurately predict how much you spend in various categories. Even the behavior of sticking to your budget will get easier, especially when you keep your why in mind.

Action Step: Schedule a date and time for your budget meeting for this month. Add it to your calendar(s) and keep your appointment like any other important scheduled event. Your budget meetings are critical for achieving your goals.

Budgeting Together

If you are married, your budget meetings must include both of you. There may be some tense moments at first, but getting through the rocky beginning together will get you to a long future with more financial freedom and comfort.

Budgeting together can strengthen your relationships. The budgeting process forces you to communicate about how you spend your money, which ultimately brings out your values and goals. You spend money on what you value, and you need to make sure your budgets add up to meet your goals.

When you set your monthly goals together, you are automatically on the same team—instead of you versus him or her. The budget you create together is like giving your promise to your spouse that you will do your part to help meet your family goals.

If you are not married, budgeting can be even easier. It is only your values you are spending money on, and it is only your goals that you are trying to achieve. You do not have to compromise or count on someone else to stick to the plan.

But budgeting by yourself also means all the glory— and all the blame—lies on you. If you do not meet your monthly budgeting goals, there is no one to blame but you.

If you want some guidance or support as you create your financial plans, you can refer back to Building Your Support Team, which is part of Step One: Laying Your Foundation. You will want to find someone willing to sit with you or Skype with you while you do your budgets. This process can strengthen your friendship, your communication, and build your confidence of handling your money.

Budgeting is also an excellent exercise to strengthen your self-control muscles and see how badly you want to get out of debt. Master this skill and you will be set to achieve your financial goals.

Action Step: Determine who will be a part of your budget meeting this month.

Permission to Spend

When people say they hate budgeting and it feels so restricting, I love Rachel Cruze's line that "Your budget gives you permission to spend." Instead of worrying if you spent too much or if you will have enough money for your next payment, your budget will spell it all out for you. If you have clearly earmarked all the money you earn, then you should know exactly how much you can spend in each category. Look at your budget as giving you permission to spend.

Now, while you're focused on rapidly getting out of debt, there probably isn't a whole lot of room for buying fun stuff in your budget. Relax! It is only for a season of life, and when it is over, you will be free to put all that money you were paying toward loans and interest toward more enjoyable things.

Budgeting Tools

There are a lot of tools available to help you with the budgeting process.

You can keep it simple with paper and pencil, use a spreadsheet to create your own budgeting template, or you can use an app or software specifically designed for budgeting.

Personally, I went from paper and pencil in the beginning to a simple electronic spreadsheet, which I still use. You might try something first then switch it up when you find something that works better too.

I use the spreadsheet to plan and track our expenses in each expense category. Then I write each month's bills on their due date on our family calendar. Keeping track of our finances is just as much a part of our daily life as appointments and birthdays. By adding our bills to our personal calendar, we are reminded to make sure enough money is in our checking account before funds are withdrawn for bills on autopay. If there is a bill we need to manually pay, the calendar reminds us to do that as well. You too might find more budgeting success by adding your bills to your personal calendar, too.

Another budgeting technique some people swear by is the "envelope system." The envelope system works like this: You allocate a certain amount, let's say $500, to your groceries expense category for the month. Then you take $500 cash, put it in an envelope labeled "Groceries," and you only buy groceries with that cash. Once the grocery cash is gone, you are done buying groceries for the month. You can do this for several categories, each with its own envelope. This helps some people stick to the amount they allocated.

With trial and error, you will figure out what works best for you as long as you do not give up. You can get instant access to the spreadsheet I use for budgeting at Bonus.TheCommonCentsClub.com.

Action Step 1: Decide which budgeting tool(s) you will use to create your budget. Will it be paper and pencil? Will it be an electronic spreadsheet? Are you going to use the envelope system? Is there an app you will use?

Action Step 2: Once you know the who, what, where, when, why, and how of the budgeting process, the next step will be to put it all together and create your own budget for next month. This budget is an essential part of your success.

Step 5. Hustle...
Then Hustle Some More

Make Your Payments Automatic

The fifth and final step to get out of debt is to **hustle...then hustle some more**! The more you hustle, the faster you will find your freedom from debt. There are lots of ways you can hustle.

The first way is to automate your student loan payments. Most lenders offer an automatic payment option where the funds are automatically pulled from your bank account on the same day every month. Some companies even offer a lower interest rate if you use the autopay option. Ideally, you would automate your minimum amount due PLUS the extra payment you decided you would put toward your loan each month to achieve your big goal. This will help keep you on track to make your debt-free dream a reality faster.

Important Tip: Make sure your extra payments go toward the loan *principal only*. Do not let the extra money go toward future payments, ever. Confirm this with your lender before you make any more extra payments or you will be prepaying interest, which is a complete waste of money. This tip is worth confirming.

Action Step: If you have not done so already, set up your automatic payments for your loans. Double check that your extra payments will go toward principal only.

Target

Now it is time to target. No, we are not going shopping! For me, that store is dangerous. We are talking about targeting one of your loans. If you have more than one loan, you might be wondering which loan you should pay extra on. Do you put a little extra toward each loan? Do you put the extra toward the smallest loan first? Do you put the extra toward the loan with the highest interest rate?

You will make the most traction if you pick one loan to focus on at a time. There are two main schools of thought for debt repayment: the "debt snowball" method and the "debt avalanche" method.

The debt snowball method is where you list your debts from smallest to largest principal (the balance). You pay the minimum amount due on all your loans except the loan with the smallest principal. All your extra payments would go to the loan with the smallest balance so you experience the triumph of eliminating one debt as fast as possible. When the smallest loan is paid off, you put all the money you were paying on the smallest loan toward your second smallest debt. You continue this approach until all your loans are paid off, paying the loan with the largest principal last.

Money gurus like Dave Ramsey and Dani Johnson recommend the debt snowball method because it works for a lot of people. This method has been shown to build confidence and keep people motivated because they see more frequent victories of eliminating one debt at a time. Because motivation is crucial for sticking to difficult plans for a fairly long period of time (most people are paying off debt for years), the debt snowball method is the more common approach.

Although I did not know it at the time, I worked the debt avalanche method. The debt avalanche plan is where you list your debts from highest interest rate to lowest interest rate. You pay the minimum amount due on all your loans, then all extra payments go toward the loan with the highest interest rate. With this method, you will pay off the debt with the highest interest rate first because that is the loan costing you the most money. When the highest interest rate loan is gone, all that money will then go toward the debt with the second highest interest rate. You will pay off the loan with the lowest interest rate last.

The debt avalanche approach is more logical because overall you pay the least amount of money to get out of debt. Since saving money and paying as little on interest as possible were key motivators for me, I targeted my largest debt first because it had the highest interest rate. But that does not necessarily mean that it is the best plan for you.

So, which method should you work? Should you pay extra on the loan with the smallest balance or the loan with the highest interest rate first?

You know yourself, your motivators, and your money habits best, so be honest with yourself and choose the method that gives you the best chance for success. The ultimate goal is to pay off your loans and get out of debt, and both plans will get you to that end goal.

Work the debt snowball method if you want more frequent victories to build your confidence, stay motivated, and stick with your plan. Work the debt avalanche method if you are motivated by numbers and know you will stick to your financial plan—even if it takes a while to pay off that first debt.

You might even start with the debt snowball method to build your confidence and establish new habits then switch to the debt avalanche method later.

Both methods require discipline and sacrifice, but both will be worth it.

Once you decide the method you are going to use, identify the one loan you will target first with your extra payments. Highlight this loan on your spreadsheet, write the balance somewhere you can see, and get after it!

Action Steps: Decide whether you will work the debt avalanche or debt snowball method. Circle it below:

Debt Snowball Debt Avalanche

Then, according to the method you chose, identify your first target loan where all your extra payments will go until it is gone! Create a nickname for the loan and write the current balance below:

Loan Nickname: _____

Loan Balance: _____

Pay Even More Whenever You Can

You figured out how much extra you can pay per month based on your budget, how fast you will pay off your loans by sticking to your plan, and set your extra monthly payment to occur automatically. This is a solid start to getting out of debt. When you want to ramp up your fight against debt yet another level, you will want to pay *even more* toward your target loan whenever you can.

Paying even more than I thought I could is how I took my goal of repaying only my *biggest loan* in *eight years* to eliminating *all* my loans in *less than three years*.

This strategy can work for you too. You will want to establish your own comfortable minimum balance for your checking account. For me, it was $1,000. I did not like my checking account to go below that, and that is what I recommend to others as well. This serves as a beginner emergency fund, so if the unexpected happens, you have cash reserves to use instead of using more debt.

As you are getting comfortable creating and sticking to a budget, you will probably find times when you have extra money in your checking account. You should be able to predict your upcoming bills, ensure they will be covered with your paychecks, then throw whatever extra money you can at your loan. So, if I had $1,300 in my checking account and had no bills due before my next payday, I logged into my student loan account and made an additional $300 payment.

This is another reason your budget is crucial to your success. You need to know how much money is coming in, and how much money is going out, to understand how much of your checking account money is extra. When you know this, you can confidently make even more extra payments and rapidly wipe out your debt.

It surprised me to find extra money in my account. I thought I was stretching my budget to the absolute limit by making my standard extra payment every month. But the truth is, the more focused on increasing my income and slashing my expenses, and the angrier I felt at the huge amount of money I was wasting on interest, the more I opened my eyes to opportunities to pay more toward my debt.

If you receive a gift of money for your birthday or Christmas, pay it (or at least half of it) toward your debt. If you get a tax return in April, pay it toward your debt. If you receive an inheritance, show the person who gifted you the money that you are financially wise and appreciative, and pay it toward your debt. Whenever you get even a slight raise or bonus at work, pay it toward your debt. Take any extra money you have, use it to lower your debt principal, and use it to dig, dig, dig out of debt.

Each extra payment may not seem like a lot at the time, but $50 here and $300 there adds up fast. If you consistently use your small financial blessings to hack away at your debt, you will be amazed at how much faster your loan principal shrinks. As you lower your principal, the amount you are charged for interest will drastically diminish too. That interest is stealing your money every month this debt sticks around.

So, maybe it is time to turn this annoying debt into a game. How fast can you wipe out your debt? You need to pay back what you borrowed, that is nonnegotiable, but how much interest you pay is up to you. I know you want to save as much as you can, so you can spend it on things you really want down the road. No matter how small the amount, whenever you can, pay even more on your debt.

Action Step: Decide what your minimum checking account balance will be. One of your goals will be to maintain this minimum balance always, cover all your bills, and pay everything above this minimum as extra payments toward your target loan.

Target Minimum Checking Account Balance:

_____

Slash Your Expenses

Slashing your expenses is another key hustling strategy. When you allow less out of your bank account, you will have more available to get out of debt.

With that burning desire to get out of debt, take a close look at your expenses. Is there anything you could remove, or at least trim? There are fourteen category ideas below of ways you might be able to reduce your spending. Some may not apply to you, while others may sound outrageous. Just keep an open mind, and I am sure you can find places to spend less money. Remember, this is temporary, and it will allow you to experience that freedom you crave.

Cable TV. Do you really need all those channels? How many channels do you actually watch? Do you need the premium package, movie channels, DVR, and on demand? Do you need cable TV, satellite TV, antenna TV, Netflix, Hulu, Sling, and Amazon Video? Can you shop around to find another option that offers what you "need" for less? Could you cut your TV expense completely?

Phone data. Can you find a cell phone company that offers new customers a deal? Can you use less data to lower your monthly bill? Can you sell your phone and buy an older one for less? Can you go without a smartphone for a while—gasp!

Coffee shop coffee. Do you need overpriced lattes? Can you brew your own cup of joe at home? Can you find recipes on Pinterest or Google to make your own latte each morning? Could you drink less coffee?

Restaurants and fast food. Can you use a gift card or coupon? Could you skip the appetizer, soda, and dessert? Can you cook dinner at home? Can you pack leftovers for lunch?

Groceries. Can you plan your meals for one week, so you only buy the food you need? Can you create a shopping list and stick to it? Could you stock up on a few essentials when there is a great deal? Can you eat the food that is already in your fridge, freezer, and pantry before buying more? Can you find a store that offers lower prices?

Liquids. Besides well water, pretty much every liquid you consume costs money. Soda. Juice. Energy drinks. Bottled water. Protein drinks. Beer. Liquor. Wine. Have you ever calculated how much you spend on liquids in a week? In a month? Could you replace your usual drink with tap water? Could you cut back on the amount you drink by even one per day?

Housing. As one of the biggest expense categories for most people, housing has the potential for the biggest savings. Could you do something extreme like find a cheaper place to live, rent out a bedroom in your house, or get a roommate to share expenses? Can you do something minor like adjust the thermometer a few degrees to save money on heat or air conditioning? Could you use a small heater or window air conditioner to heat or cool just one room rather than the entire house?

Pets. I know pets are a beloved part of many families, mine included, but they are also expensive. The food, gear, grooming, vet bills, and even kennel costs add up. If it is not too late, promise yourself you will not get a pet and add another ongoing expense to your life until you have paid off your debt. Perhaps you can use a pet as a motivator and get one when you pay off your loans early. If you already have a pet, can you find a way to reduce these expenses?

Vehicles. Are car payments one of your monthly expenses? Could you get by with an older or less flashy vehicle? I dare you to calculate how much faster you could pay off your student loans if you did not have car payments. If you sold your current vehicle and bought (not financed) a cheaper one, you could put all that car payment money toward your target debt instead. I detest car payments for the same reasons I cannot stand student loan payments: it is money down the drain on interest; it is another thing bought that you could not afford; it is payments on something going down in value; and it is keeping the unnecessary strain of payments in your life for years to come. Can you get nasty car payments out of your life?

Transportation. Can you get by with one less vehicle? Can you do all your errands in one trip rather than making a different trip every day? Can you walk, bike, or carpool? When you walk, bike, or carpool, you are less likely to stop at a store and buy something on your way. Changes in transportation could save you gas, wear, and maintenance on your vehicle too.

Insurance. When was the last time you shopped around for lower insurance rates? Can you find cheaper rates for your auto, home, renter's, life, health, or dental insurance? You will first want to speak to a professional to determine if your current insurance coverage is enough, too little, or too much. Then shop around for the best price. It is possible you could get a lower rate for the same coverage through a different insurance company.

Entertainment. Can you skip the concerts, ball games, and weekend trips? Could you borrow a movie or use a coupon code for a free Redbox rental instead of going to the theatre? Can you play games or have a bonfire with friends at home instead of going out? Could you go out to eat for breakfast rather than dinner?

Library. When was the last time you used the public library? It is an often-overlooked FREE resource for internet, books, music, movies, children's classes, book clubs, and more. Before you spend money on these things, check to see what your local library offers.

Giving. Giving is commendable, but are there ways you can give while spending less money? Can you volunteer your time instead of an item as a gift? Can you make a handmade greeting card instead of buying one? Can you reuse gift bags and tissue paper? Can you wrap your dad's present in newspaper? (I did! He did not mind.)

I hope that helped you find at least one new way you could save money each month. If you are struggling to pick which nonessential (but oh, so comforting) expense you are willing to cut, try ranking them. Keep the ones you like best and cut the ones at the bottom of the list. Remember, this is only until you get out of debt. It is not forever!

In addition, here are three more strategies you can practice to spend less money in general:

Wait thirty days. If you run out of toilet paper and need some today, please, go ahead and buy some. On the other hand, if you are enticed by anything that is not a necessity (e.g., a new shirt) wait thirty days before you buy it. This makes you exercise your self-control muscle, allows you to determine if you love it, and gives you time to verify if it fits into your budget. This method will drastically reduce impulse buys that you later regret.

Add a zero. Before you purchase something, mentally add a zero to its price tag and ask yourself if you would still buy the item. Why? Because that represents how much you could earn if you were to invest that money (like in a retirement account), or how much you could save on interest if you were to pay off debt with that money instead.

No spend days. Start with one day per month and dedicate it as a day you will not spend *any* money. Eat the food in your kitchen. Wear the clothes in your closet. Stay home for the evening or walk to a place for free. No matter what, keep your money and your plastic cards locked up for the day. Eventually, try dedicating one day per week as a no spend day, and you will spend even less money during the month.

I could go on and on with ways to spend less money. Wash your own car. Learn to change your own oil. Stop buying lottery tickets. Quit smoking. Buy generic brands. The point is to get started by picking one of these ideas and focus on it. Commit to it and make it a new habit. Then add another. Over time you will be surprised at how drastically you can slash your expenses if you are diligent about how you spend your hard-earned money.

When you find money to save in your budget, put *all* that money toward your target loan immediately. The longer you wait to put extra payments toward your debt, the more time you have to accidentally spend it on something else instead. The point here is to spend less so you can pay more on your debt.

Action Step: Review your expenses and start slashing. Pick at least one expense **category** you will focus on for the next month so you can spend less, save more, and eliminate your debt even faster.

Starting next month, I will cut my expenses in the following category(ies): _____, _____, _____,

Then identify one **strategy** you will use to spend less money in general, such as waiting thirty days, adding a zero, or selecting a no spend day.

And I will use this strategy to spend less money _____.

Boost Your Income

When you are on a mission to rapidly pay off your debt, you should always be on the lookout for ways to earn extra money. Every day you should be hustlin'! How can you can make more money? Answer: there are a bazillion ways!

I love Dave Ramsey's saying, "A great place to go when you're broke is to work." And when you are in student loan debt, you are broke. You still have not paid for your education expenses. Your student loan debt will not go away even with bankruptcy. That means it is time to hustle that debt away, watch fewer hours of TV, and spend more hours working.

There are three general ways to boost your income: 1) Earn more money for your current working hours; 2) Work more hours; 3) Sell your stuff.

Your Current Job

The first place to look for extra money is your current job. Earning more money for the hours you already work is the wisest way to increase your income because it does not require any additional time. If you are a rock star employee, consider brushing up on your negotiation skills and asking for a raise. However, before you ask for a raise, make sure it is clear how you offer more value to your employer now than when your current wage was determined.

A second way to earn more from your current job is to brainstorm ways you can take on more responsibilities. Most bosses will be happy to thank you with higher pay when you take something off their list of responsibilities.

A third way is to see if you can work more hours for your current employer. This makes sense if more hours worked equals more money in your paycheck, so this method may not apply if you are a salaried employer. If overtime pay is an option at your place of employment, cha-ching! Grab as many of those hours as you can. Offer to pick up shifts whenever someone needs time off. You may become the VIP to your co-workers and boss during this time. Your evenings and weekends might include more hours of work and less hours of play, but it is only temporary, and this is a proven way you can earn more money.

Add Another Job

After you exhaust your options for your current employer, keep looking. You can get another job working for someone else or start your own small business. It does not matter if you are a teacher or lawyer, you can mow lawns, deliver pizzas, or clean houses for extra cash. You can babysit, dog-sit, or house-sit. There are always people looking for help and willing to pay for it—you just have to find them. Even Craigslist has random jobs posted like "looking for help moving this weekend," "looking for yard work help," or "looking for someone to run weekly errands." These may not pay a fortune, but they are ways to put extra cash in your pocket.

You can also start your own small business. Use a talent you already have or invest in yourself and learn a new skill. Reading or watching videos can teach you numerous skills you can use to serve others. Refinishing old furniture, making baby blankets, power washing decks, teaching English online...the options are endless.

Caution Consultants

As you are contemplating possible side jobs to boost your income, here is a word of caution: be careful about side hustles as a consultant for the clothing, trendy bags, essential oils, personal care products, weight loss, kitchen gadget companies, and so on.

It seems a lot of people find a product they love and become a consultant to sell the product. Usually this consultant role serves to help others, share a product you adore, and earn some extra money. Sounds great, right?

Well, what I have discovered is these can often be traps that get you to spend more money. If you are required to spend money just to keep your points, earn a discount, or get "free" products, you may actually be *spending* more money instead of *earning* more money!

There are rare exceptions. If you are indeed earning a profit, which is above and beyond what you put back into the business, then it should show up as extra income in your budget that you can use to pay off debt. If that is the case, you may have a legitimate business as a consultant. Congrats!

However, if what you are really gaining is more stuff, and you are continuously spending the money you earn to get more stuff, then it is time to find a different way to boost your income. That does not mean you must stop doing it. But it does mean you should stop pretending your time and effort as a consultant is producing more income. While digging out of debt, it is important your valuable time is spent earning more money you can use to repay your debt.

Sell Your Stuff

Another way you can earn more money is to sell your stuff. Before you dismiss this idea thinking you do not have anything to sell, listen up. You do. If you take a good hard look in your closets, drawers, shelves, garage, attic, and basement, I am willing to bet you have something you can sell. An extra vehicle—cha-ching! Those fifteen shirts you cringe at in your closet—sell them! That tool in the garage you have not used in three years—someone will buy it! The treadmill hiding under a layer of dust—stop swearing you will use it tomorrow and swap it for cash!

If you look around your place and still do not think you have anything to sell, then I wonder why you are so attached to *stuff*? Is holding onto all those things worth the bondage of keeping debt in your life? Do you even remember what is inside all those plastic totes? If you have not used something in the past year, and it does not bring you immense joy, sell it. Put it on Craigslist, Facebook buy & sell groups, Etsy, farmer's markets, eBay, or have a rummage sale.

I do not know why it is so hard for many of us to get rid of our stuff. Maybe it means we regret the purchase, or maybe we fear needing it "someday," but I do know stuff does not equal happiness. *Less* stuff may even bring you *more* joy because you can focus on the things you use and enjoy, and stop wasting energy on the clutter. Selling your stuff and having extra money to put toward your debt is like having your cake and eating it too. You can have less clutter, less debt, and more happiness.

Every Little Bit Counts

Do not despair even if you cannot negotiate a big raise, put in 20 hours of overtime each week, or sell something huge. Do whatever you can to earn just a little more money than you are earning now. Every little bit adds up. Most debt payoff success stories don't involve a $20,000 raise. Rather, most debt payoff success stories include many small mindset and behavior changes, which are applied consistently until the end goal is achieved.

Your small sacrifices now are what will help make your big dreams later become your reality. Your student loans will be gone if you stick to this plan. You get to decide how fast you knock out that debt by hustling...then hustling some more.

Action Step: What is one thing you can do this week to boost your income through your current job, another job, or by selling stuff? _____.

What is another thing you can do in the next six months to boost your income even more? _____.

The 5 Steps Recap

Here is a recap of the five essential steps to quickly pay off your student loans:

1. Lay a solid foundation

2. Know where you are

3. Know where you want to go

4. The *B* word

5. Hustle...then hustle some more

If you follow these five steps, your debt and the burden it brings to your life will be gone. In the next section, Part 3, we will cover extra things you can do to have a more successful journey out of debt.

Part 3:
The Extras

"If you want something you've never had,
you must be willing to do something you've never done.
-Thomas Jefferson

Beyond the 5 Steps

You can go above and beyond the five key steps to achieve debt-free success by finding ways to **stay motivated**, **continue learning**, and **avoid costly mistakes**.

Learning is considered an extra step because it is ongoing and these topics are optional, whereas the five-step plan we covered is nonnegotiable. Also, it can take a while to learn about all the programs and weigh your options, and I do not want you to get so wrapped up learning about *everything* that you delay taking action on *anything*. After you master the five basic steps, take time to research and see what applies to your situation. The topics you will want to learn about are consolidation, refinancing, reimbursement, and forgiveness programs.

Keep Learning

Debt Consolidation

Consolidation is combining multiple loans into one. It is optional. It is often used to make payments easier, so you can make one payment instead of several. While this is a perk, it should not be the primary reason you consolidate.

Consolidating your student loans is a wise option to consider if you can get a lower interest rate. Otherwise, you should just stick to making multiple payments and use that annoyance as a motivator to pay them off, one by one, as fast as possible.

Sometimes people want to consolidate loans because they feel like they are eliminating loans. Don't be fooled. If you consolidate, you are not eliminating loans. You are taking your loans from several smaller buckets and lumping them into one bigger bucket. The amount of debt you owe is the same. It is the interest rate that typically changes. If you research your options and find that you can get a lower interest rate by consolidating your loans, and there are no adverse stipulations in the fine print, then consolidation could help you repay less overall.

Refinance

Refinancing means you finance your loans, typically with a new loan at a lower interest rate. Like consolidation, the only reason refinancing could help is if you can get a lower interest rate.

With a lower interest rate, your monthly bill should be lower. This means if you pay the same amount you were paying before refinancing, a greater percentage of your payment goes toward your principal. This also means you will pay off your loan quicker.

Before refinancing, diligently research or seek help from a professional financial advisor. Many lenders have fees associated with refinancing, and you will want to ensure these fees do not cost more than what you would save with the lower interest rate.

SoFi (SoFi.com) is a refinancing company I have seen recommended numerous times by other student loan borrowers. I have a good friend who got a much lower interest rate by refinancing through them. At the time of this writing, SoFi reportedly has no fees and their advertised interest rate is less than half the rate I had. My unique referral link is sofi.com/share/271811. If you use this link to refinance your student loans, you get $100 bonus, and I get a perk for the referral. Thank you in advance if you use my link, and let me know if you do. I would love to connect and hear how it helps you.

Regrettably, I did not use SoFi simply because I did not know about them until after my loans were repaid. If I still had student loans, however, SoFi would be the first place I would look for more information because I now have learned refinancing could save you *thousands* of dollars. How? Let's pretend you have $30,000 in student loans. You have a 6.8% interest rate, and you are on a 10-year repayment plan. Your monthly payments are $345, and you will end up repaying $41,774.21 total.

After defining your why and squeezing your budget tighter, you decided you are going to pay $300 extra every month toward the principal. Your monthly payments are now $645. You end up repaying only $34,919.21 total by making payments for 55 months, instead of 120 months. This plan will save you $6,855 in interest and 5.4 years of payments.

However, let's pretend you find a company that will refinance your student loans and give you a new loan at a 3% rate of interest. That same $645 payment each month will eliminate your $30,000 loan in 50 payments, and cost a total of only $31,933.47. While this lower interest rate only equals five fewer payments, it would save you $3,000 in interest!

This is not a far-fetched example, and it demonstrates how adding consistent extra payments and a lower interest rate could save you $10,000 dollars. Seriously, *ten grand!* What would you rather do with $10,000 than throw it away as interest payments for a decade? I can think of a lot of things, and I know you can too.

This example also shows the major reduction in payoff time that comes with the extra principal payments. With the standard repayment plan with the standard interest rate, you would make payments for 120 months, or ten years. With the accelerated repayment plan and a lower interest rate, you would make payments for only 50 months, or just over four years.

Things that lower your interest rate, like refinancing, allow you to pay more toward your principal, so do your research and take advantage of them when you can.

Reimbursement

Reimbursement is repaying someone for money they spent. More employers are realizing the enormous amount of student loan debt many people are facing.

Employers are also realizing student loan reimbursement is one way to attract and retain quality employees. While it is not yet commonplace, more and more employers are adding this benefit for its employees.

Because this information changes by the day, I am not going to list specific participating companies in a book. However, I do encourage you to research and ask questions. Even if your employer does not currently offer reimbursement, sharing that such a benefit would help reduce employees' financial stress and increase employees' funds for things like retirement investing may be enough for your boss to start such a program.

There are also companies that offer prepaid tuition programs. This means they will actually prepay your college tuition if you earn a degree toward an in-demand field. The United States Armed Forces have special loan repayment programs for qualified students as well.

While I would not count on reimbursement or pre-paid tuition as your method for getting out of debt, it is worth considering to see if it applies.

Forgiveness

There have also been loan forgiveness programs where your loans are forgiven as a benefit for your service in certain careers. Most of the program details depend on the type of loan you have and the type of position you hold. Positions that have most commonly qualified for forgiveness programs include Peace Corps volunteers, teachers of certain subjects and/or teachers in low-income schools, law enforcement or corrections officers, child or family services workers, Head Start workers, nurses or medical technicians, and professional providers of early intervention services.

As with most government programs, these change over time. You can visit a website like https://studentaid .ed.gov/sa/repay-loans/forgiveness-cancellation to find out if you qualify for any current loan forgiveness programs. Meeting all the requirements for loan forgiveness is rare, but not impossible. Just be sure to examine all the details of what will be forgiven and what requirements must be met first before you count on forgiveness to remove your student loans.

If you research and find you qualify for loan for-giveness after a few years of service, congrats! It is a perk of your service, so enjoy it. However, I do not recommend counting on a new government program to forgive your debt ten years down the road. For starters, you will want to get rid of your student loans before then. Second, you never know when forgiveness programs will change or be cancelled. Instead, keep your financial future within your control by tightening your budget, increasing your income, and hustling your loans away by following the plan that is proven to work.

Stay Motivated

Revisit Your Why, Your Goals, and Your Progress Each Month

For some, getting started on a debt payoff plan is the hardest part. For others, it is staying motivated during the long, jarring ride.

I remember being super motivated in the beginning of my journey because I found a smarter way to handle my debt, and also near the end once my biggest loan dipped below $10,000 because I knew I could sprint to the finish line. But in the middle of the debt repayment, there were lots of times I felt the whole situation was unfair and ridiculous. It seemed like I was never going to win this battle against my debt. It was tempting to bail and give up. You might experience similar feelings.

To keep yourself on track and resist the urge to give up, revisit your why, your goals, and your progress each month. Perhaps you can start your monthly budget meetings by reviewing these things. They can remind you *why* you are working so hard to boost your income, *why* you are keeping a strict budget, and *why* you are having the budget meeting in the first place. It can be motivating to review your progress to remind yourself that the plan works—so stick with it. Revisit your why, your goals, and your progress again whenever you are feeling low, tempted to impulsively buy something, or take a spontaneous vacation to help you stay on track.

Immerse Yourself in Success Stories

Reading or listening to success stories of others who have already accomplished what you are working to achieve—a life without student loan debt—is another way to spark your motivation.

I read articles like "How one woman paid off $70,000 in debt in five years," and listened to debt-free screams on *The Dave Ramsey Show*. These are the type of inspirational stories I hope to collect and share with others as well. Success stories can inspire others to believe they can do it too, and they can help people stick to their goals even when it gets incredibly tough.

So, when you pay off your student loans, I would LOVE to hear your story. Why keep your story to yourself when you can use it to help and motivate others? You can connect with me at TheCommonCentsClub.com to share your story anytime.

Celebrate Wins Along the Way

Celebrating memorable milestones along your debt payoff journey is another way to keep yourself motivated. Use common sense and celebrate with small rewards to avoid derailing your progress, but find a way to celebrate somehow. It is okay to acknowledge your sacrifice and hard work to overcome your debt and achieve a better future. Celebrate your wins...then keep hustlin'!

Find Your Tribe

Another way to stay motivated is to surround yourself with others on a similar mission as you. Getting people around you who can relate to the hustling and sacrifices you are making in pursuit of freedom from your debt can be comforting. It can make your new "weird" lifestyle feel more normal.

Maybe you are lucky enough to find people who share your personal finance goals and values at work, in your family, or in your community. Some places of employment or churches even offer money management classes, such as Financial Peace University. These classes can offer accountability and a strong sense of community because you are all striving for a better financial situation. You are all focused on eliminating debt from your life. And you are all going through it together.

You can also find a tribe of people online. You do not need to know people personally to reap the benefits of having a supportive community. You can find thousands of people online trying to get out of debt just like you. You might subscribe to blogs like ThePennyHoarder.com, MakingSenseofCents.com, LivingWellSpendingLess.com, SmartPassiveIncome.com, or SideHustleNation.com to learn new ideas for cutting expenses and earning more money. Most of these online communities have Facebook groups where you can connect with other people who are on a similar financial journey as you.

No matter where you find your people, find others to help keep you motivated.

A Dozen Deadly Mistakes

What NOT to Do

Now that you know what TO DO, I will briefly touch on a dozen things NOT TO DO. These are common myths and mistakes which destroy debt-free dreams every day.

Taking on More Debt

Taking on more debt when you are trying to pay off the debt you already have only makes your battle against debt harder. Do not sign a car loan, payday loan, or title loan. Do not open another credit card no matter what the rewards are. Do not finance new furniture or appliances. Do not finance more college credits because you already have student loans anyway. Your focus should be 100% on cutting your expenses, increasing your income, and eliminating your loans. Avoid all kinds of debt like a nasty disease so you can soon experience the peace of debt-free life.

Consolidating for Ease, Not Logic

Consolidating for the ease of having one payment, rather than consolidating for a lower interest rate, can actually hurt you financially. If you combine loans that have a lower interest rate with loans that have a higher interest rate, you could end up increasing the total amount you pay in interest. Ensure the numbers make sense and only consolidate your loans to gain a lower interest rate.

Not Refinancing

I mentioned before that not refinancing is a mistake I made. If companies like SoFi existed when I was paying off my debt, I did not know about them. Refinancing could have saved me several thousand dollars. Of course, do your own research and only choose a reputable company. You may be able to find one without a bunch of fees that will offer you a remarkably lower interest rate. A couple hours of researching could save you several thousand dollars.

Having Too Many Targets

Another common mistake is trying to attack too many debts at once. Just like multitasking, when you try to do too many things at once, you do not do any of it well. Pick one loan and focus on it. Pay your minimum payments on the rest and attack the one target loan like it will kill you if you do not kill it first. In a way, it will. Debt kills the freedom to create your dream life.

Similarly, trying to pay off your student loans while saving for kids' college, investing in your retirement, and saving to buy a home is also sending your money in too many directions at once. Instead, attack your debt first, then switch your focus to something like saving for a new home or investing for retirement. Getting out of debt as soon as possible is one of the best things you can do for, and model for, your kids. So, hold off on your kids' college savings until your own college expenses are paid for first. If you annihilate your loans, you can save thousands in interest. The thousands of dollars you save in interest can be used to invest in things like a home, retirement, or college savings later.

Riding the Lazy River of Minimum Payments

Riding the lazy river of minimum payments for decades and paying thousands more than you need to in interest is not a wise way to spend your money. Instead of making your debt payoff a lazy river ride, make it a fast and intense roller coaster ride. Add sharp turns in your behavior. Create intense drops in your expenses. Make your debt repayment a memorable ride that you are proud of, and one that is worth talking about in the future.

Paying Ahead Interest

Paying ahead interest is another mathematical mistake. Make sure all your additional payments go toward your debt principal only. By default, some companies will apply your extra payments to future interest. This favors the lender, not you. Make sure you only pay extra on your principal to eliminate your debt as fast as possible.

Caving to Bad Customer Service

Do not be surprised if you encounter unfriendly or incompetent customer service along your way. And do not let that poor service deter you from crushing your debt.

In my three-year journey, I had to deal with plenty of pain-in-the-butt phone calls and multiple online glitches. Although I set up automatic extra payments each month and they sent me a letter confirming the change, my lender continuously withdrew the wrong amount from my checking account on unpredictable days of the month. Instead of letting these errors by the lending company get in the way of achieving my goal, I was persistent, sacrificed the .25% reduction in interest for automatic payments, and did it the manual way.

Loan companies do not always make it easy for you to pay extra, but be persistent anyway. Ask questions, get documentation and clarification, fight through the frustrations, and stick to your plan. Let nothing get in your way.

Assuming Others Have Your Best Interest in Mind

Another common mistake is assuming someone else has your best interest in mind, such as the federal education department, the financial aid office at your university, or the bank. These places have many nice and helpful employees. However, they are in the business of making money on interest by lending you money. Bigger loans, higher interest rates, and longer repayment periods lead to more money in their pocket—and less in yours.

Here is a prime example: I received a statement from the federal student loan department every month during my repayment period. On the front of every statement, in a carefully worded way, I was reminded that there were other repayment plans that could lower my monthly payments. It was written in a way that emphasized the benefits I could experience with a different payment plan. Why stick with the standard repayment plan when I could have lower payments every month with a different plan? However, all the other repayment plans would have cost me more overall. Most would have kept me in debt for years—or even decades—longer. All those options that "benefited me" looked shiny on the surface, but in reality, they would have cost me more money overall. No, thank you.

You may receive similar suggestions. Be sure to do your own research and use your common sense to create your best plan of action. Be careful not to assume a lender has your best interest in mind.

Being Near Temptations

Have you ever tried to go on a diet, eat healthier, or lose weight? Me too. You know the old advice to keep junk food out of the house because if it is in the house, you are going to eat it. It is so true! When I put junk food in my shopping cart, I know it is eventually going to end up in my belly. So, when I am serious about eating healthier, the junk food cannot come into my house. It is tempting and requires my self-control muscles to work extra hard.

The same thing is true when you are on a financial diet. Recognize where you are tempted to cheat (aka spend money) and stay away.

One of my strategies was that I no longer went to the mall or stores to browse. If I went shopping, it was with a list that I stuck to, and I usually researched to find the lowest price ahead of time. One of the best "tricks" I learned was that the best way to save money at Kohl's was by NOT using that 30% off coupon. In fact, I save *100%* when I do not go to the store at all.

Another way to more easily resist temptation is to unsubscribe from store emails, newsletters, and magazines. I have unsubscribed from a lot of store emails, and I do not miss any of them. But I am not perfect. For the few stores I might need a coupon for someday, and I cannot get myself to unsubscribe from, I create a filter to automatically archive the emails. The advertisement emails skip my inbox, so I never see them. If I ever need to buy something from that store, I can still easily search the archives of my email to find the latest deal. I started this practice years ago and I rarely recall digging out an archived email for this purpose. Probably twice. And I have avoided buying *many* things simply because I do not see the "limited time, super-duper savings offer for VIP customers only!"

Finally, when you get ads in the mail, feel free to toss them without looking through them. If you are like me, when you browse advertisements, you are suddenly reminded of all the stuff you "need" to make your house, wardrobe, kids, pets, or life better. For this period of time when you are committed to erasing your debt, just avoid these temptations too.

Using Repayment Plans to Lower Your Payments

If you find yourself struggling to make your minimum payments, your time and energy should be on cutting your expenses and increasing your income like your life depends on it. Because it does!

Unless there is absolutely no other option, avoid the trap of any repayment plan other than the standard plan. Repayment plans that lower your monthly payment are not a gift. Plans with lower monthly payments keep you in debt longer and steal even more of your hard-earned money for bogus interest over time.

For example, the PAYE (Pay As You Earn) repayment program stretches your ten-year repayment plan out to twenty-five years! It more than doubles the amount of time you will be stuck living with student loan payments.

Your goal is to pay your student loans off faster. To do this, you will want to be on the standard repayment plan, consistently paying extra each month, and paying even more whenever you can. So, if you are on a different repayment plan, do what you need to do to get on the standard plan. This will help you get out of debt the fastest.

Believing in "Good Debt"

Have you heard that there is "good debt"? This is a myth I used to believe. However, after years of student loan payments and looking at the interest on our home mortgage, I am not sure what is "good" about them. I look forward to being completely debt-free someday!

The root of *freedom* is *free*. And who doesn't love free? Free from the shackles of debt. Free from payments. Free from ridiculous fees and interest. Free to say you own everything you have. Free from the burden and stress of debt. Free from owing anything to anyone. That's what I call good.

I understand a college education without student loans may not be possible for many people. I was in that situation too. So, the investment and opportunity of the college education was probably a good thing. But keeping those loans around for decades as a reminder that you borrowed thousands of dollars for your education...that's not a good thing. Paying thousands upon thousands in interest...that's not a good thing either.

Now that you have the student loans, use that educated brain to wake up and destroy your debt.

Hoping for Forgiveness

Hoping for a federal program to forgive your student loans sounds like an unwise plan to me. More than likely, the federal government played a large role in getting you into your student loan mess. It was the federal government who recently approved people for massive loans, more than doubled the student loan interest rates, and spiked college tuition costs across the country. Do you really trust those same people to now magically get you (and millions of others) out of debt? Since interest is a huge money maker, do you think they truly want you out of debt?

Heck, our government cannot even find their own way out of debt. Furthermore, with the swing in politics from one party leader to the next, you never know what policy or program changes will happen one, five, or ten years from now. It is far too risky for me to recommend counting on a lofty loan forgiveness program to stick around and work as promised.

Instead, knock out your debt yourself. Take ownership of the money you borrowed. Get motivated. Lay your solid foundation. Figure out exactly where you are financially. Set super SMART goals and determine where you want to go. Become a budgeting master. Hustle every day and pay extra whenever you can. Keep learning and stay motivated until the end. Dare to be different. Dare to be amazing. Dare to pay off your debt so fast others will ask, "How did you do that?"

What Will Your Story Be?

You Decide

Now, the most significant question is: What will *your* story be?

It is your turn to pay your student loans, get out of debt, and be free to live your dream life. You have the knowledge and step-by-step plan to get out of debt. You have proof that you do not need a six-figure income or to move to another country to repay your loans. But knowledge and proof are not enough. The real change happens when you apply that knowledge and follow the steps in your own life. Start with Step One and move through the steps, implementing each action item along the way. You CAN do it! You, your future, and your dreams are worth it.

The decisions you make today affect your situation tomorrow. Your story can not only be something that fills you with pride, but it can also inspire others who feel financially helpless or lost. Be proof that breaking free from your student loans can be done.

You decide today what your story will be.

Grateful for You

Leave a Review

Thank you so much for reading my book. I am humbled and grateful for you and your time.

People love finding and reading books with a lot of great reviews, so if you found this book helpful, informative, or inspiring, **will you please take 60 seconds and leave a review for my book**? Your review can help someone else who is trying to get out of debt find my book and resources. Each and every review makes a difference.

Refer A Friend

Do you know a family member, co-worker, neighbor, or friend with student loans? Let them know about this book. You can tell them about it, let them borrow your book, or buy them a copy of their own. One simple book could change their life.

Email Me & Free Resources

Finally, feel free to email me any time, no matter where you are in your debt journey. Whether you have questions, found something especially helpful, or want to share your story, I want to hear about it! Email me at **Val@TheCommonCentsClub.com**.

You can also download your free bonus resources—including my personal budgeting template and a checklist to guide you every step of the way—at: Bonus.TheCommonCentsClub.com to jumpstart your debt-free journey. I hope to hear from you soon. Every review, referral, and email means the world to me.

Let your light shine,

-Val Breit

Acknowledgments

My story and this book would not have been possible without my husband, who gives unwavering support, encouragement, and belief in me. Your sacrifice, teamwork, and love for our family makes living my dream a reality every day.

This journey would not have been the same without my sisters, who have been incredible role models as college grads, stay-at-home moms, and successful entrepreneurs. Thank you for being amazing women to look up to.

I never would have written this book had my brother-in-law not introduced me to self-publishing and being an online entrepreneur. Thank you to The Dude at Kindlepreneur.com.

I am also incredibly grateful for my sisters and mom, who read my first (very rough) draft and gave invaluable feedback whenever I needed it. I knew you all were good writers, but I did not know you were fantastic writers! Thank you for sharing your talent and time. Please write your own books someday, and I am happy to return the favor.

I also appreciate the book launch crew in The Common Cents Club Facebook group for your encouragement and helpful insight along the way. You are a fun group, and I cannot wait to hear more debt payoff success stories.

Finally, I am thankful for you for reading this book and sharing your precious time. Thank you.

Made in the USA
Middletown, DE
18 December 2018